Edward O'Brien
Mural Artist
1910–1975

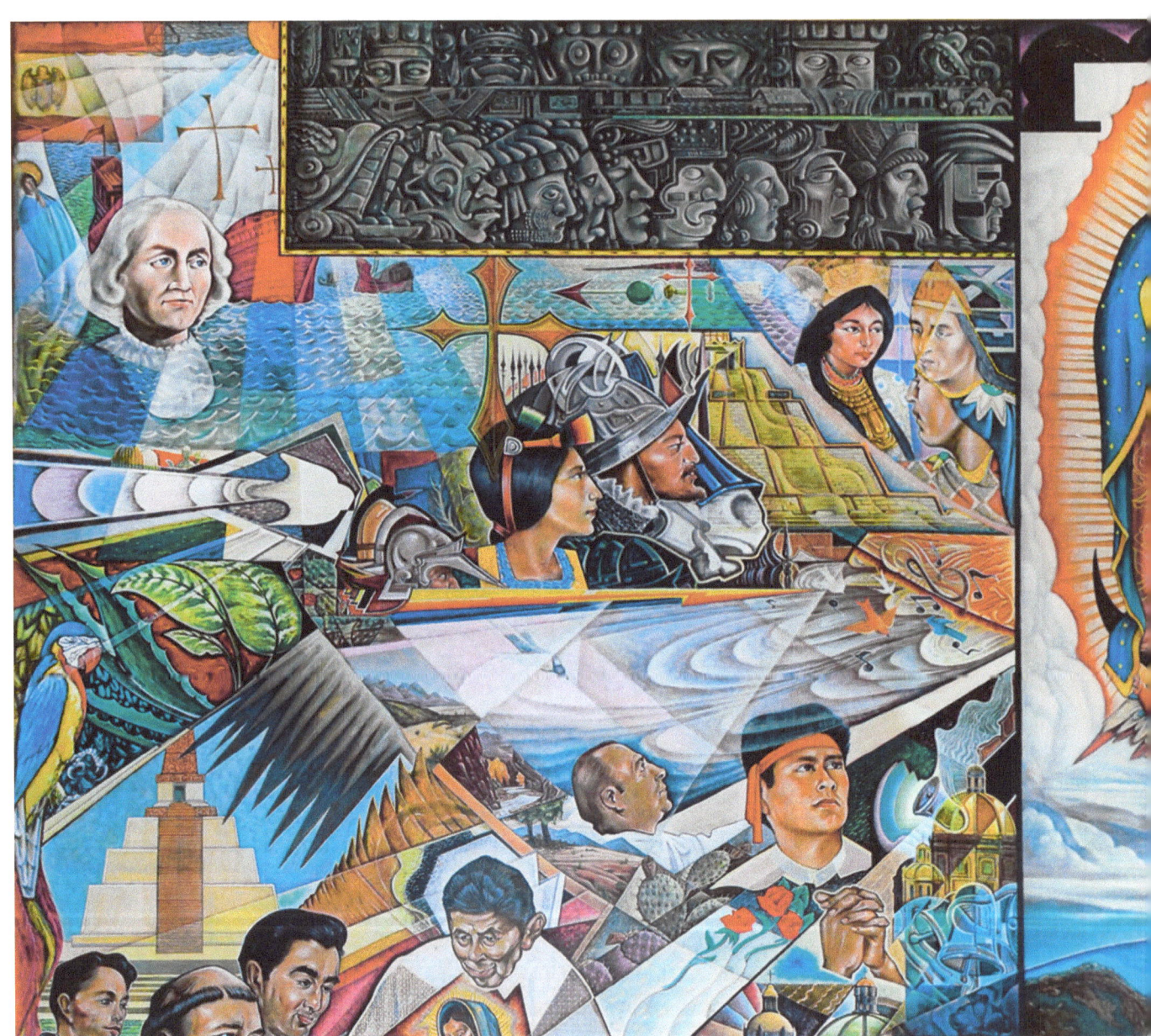

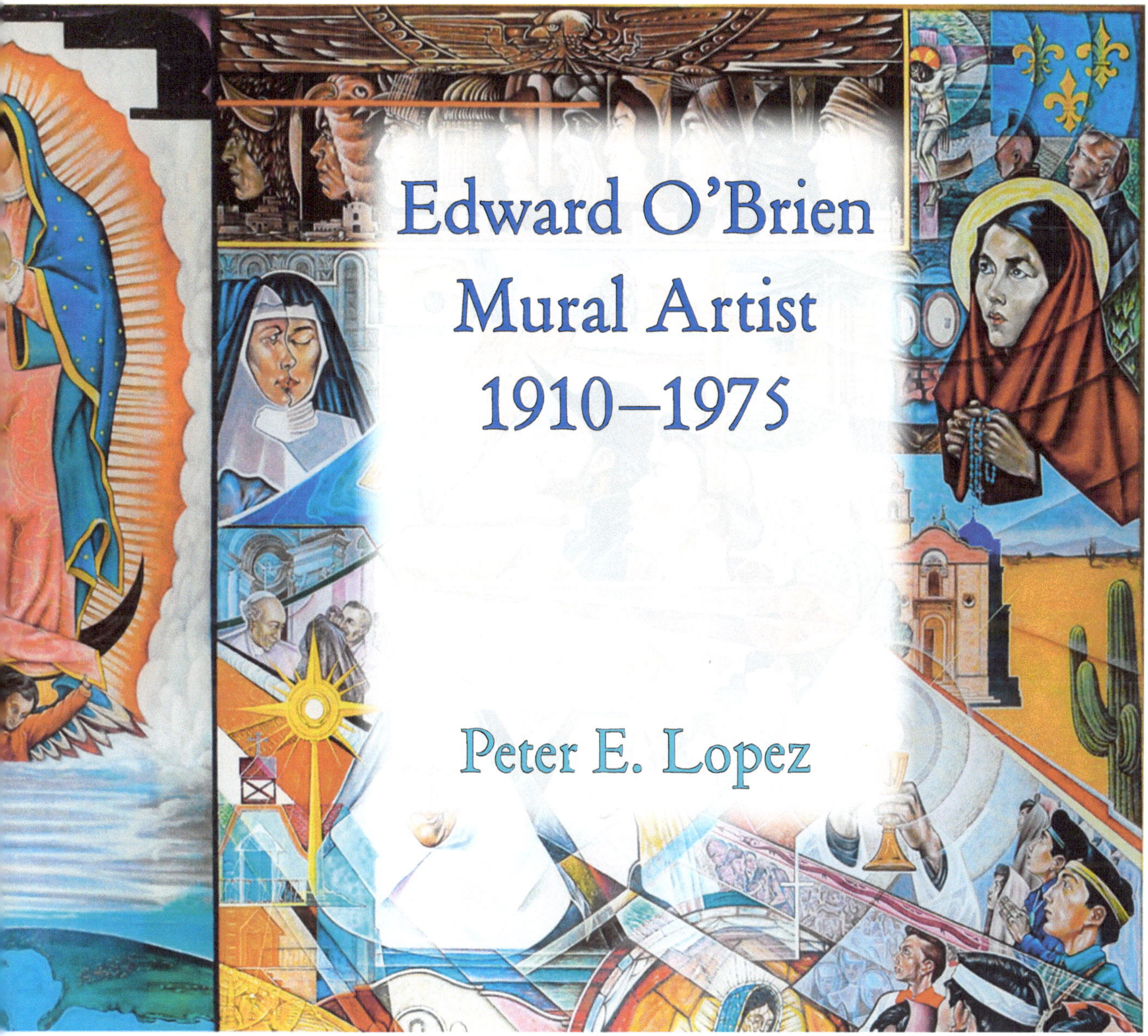

Edward O'Brien
Mural Artist
1910–1975

Peter E. Lopez

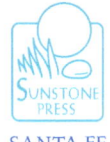

SUNSTONE
PRESS

SANTA FE

Sunstone books may be purchased for educational, business, or sales promotional use.
For information please write: Special Markets Department, Sunstone Press,
P.O. Box 2321, Santa Fe, New Mexico 87504-2321.

Book and Cover design › Vicki Ahl
Body typeface › Poliphilus MT Pro
Printed on acid-free paper
∞

Library of Congress Cataloging-in-Publication Data

Lopez, Peter E., 1940-
  Edward O'Brien, mural artist : 1910-1975 / by Peter E. Lopez.
      pages cm
  ISBN 978-0-86534-933-9 (softcover : alk. paper)
  1. Painters--United States--Biography. I. O'Brien, Edward, 1910-1975. II. Title.
  ND237.O345L67 2012
  759.13--dc23
  [B]
                                      2012048625

WWW.SUNSTONEPRESS.COM
SUNSTONE PRESS / POST OFFICE BOX 2321 / SANTA FE, NM 87504-2321 /USA
(505) 988-4418 / ORDERS ONLY (800) 243-5644 / FAX (505) 988-1025

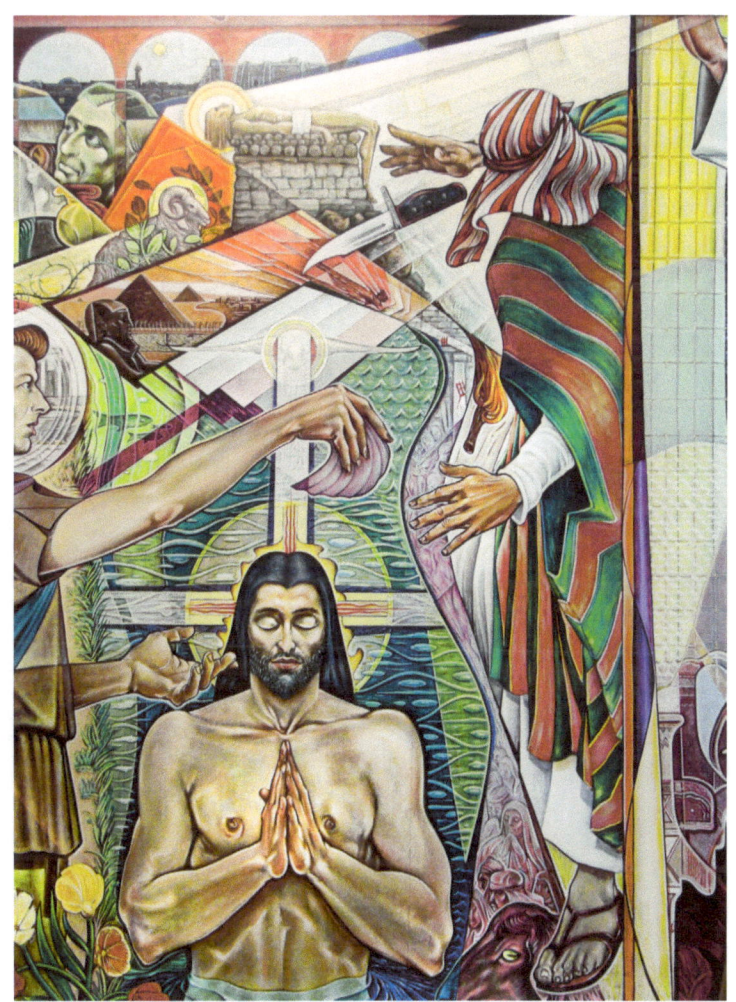

Detail from *Christ in Man* page 41

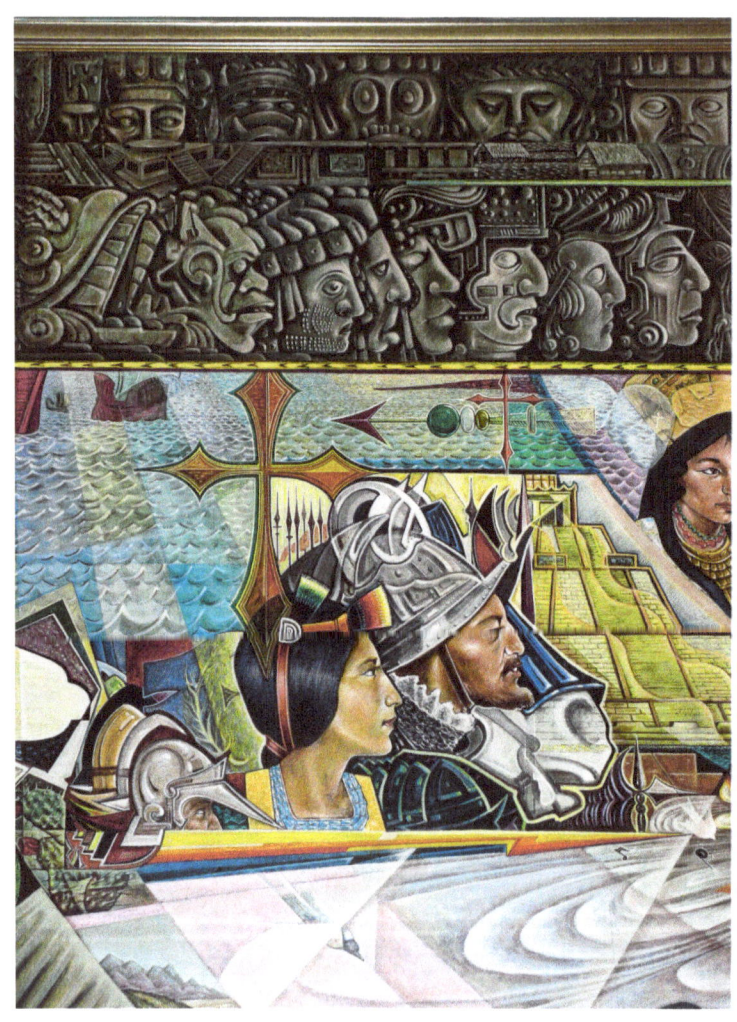

Detail from *Our Lady of Guadalupe's Love for the Indian Race* (1966) page 37

Contents

Preface

On the summer of 2009, I decided to take a break from my career as a santero artist to explore another avenue of creativity. I was not sure what would happen but, sometimes in my life, when I have sought change, a new challenge has presented itself. The seeds that led to my research into the life of Edward O'Brien were sown by a phone call from my sister, Lenore Bockbrader. She had a home-design client, Barbara Tafoya, who wanted an artist to paint a rendition of a mural that was in the main building of the closed St. Catherine's Indian School in Santa Fe, New Mexico on the property the Tafoya family owned.

Barbara Tafoya and I met at the school site so that I could view and photograph the mural for a possible art commission. As we walked into the main building's corridor and opened the door to the first room on the right, the room was in total darkness. The electricity was cut off and the windows were boarded to protect the building. Barbara had a flashlight but I requested that we remove the covering of the windows from the outside. She agreed and we went outside and removed the wooden panels and set them aside.

When we returned to the room, sunlight was streaming through the windows onto the twenty by ten foot mural that stood before us. There was complete silence between Barbara and me as we gazed upon the mural. I was in awe of the magnificent work of art before me. The mural depicted history and religion expressed by an eclectic mixture of landscapes, portraits and architecture. At the center of the mural was the image of "Our Lady of Guadalupe." I asked Barbara Tafoya: "Who painted this mural?" She replied, "Edward O'Brien."

The mural was produced in the year 1965 and completed in early 1967. St. Catherine's Industrial Indian School was founded in the late nineteenth century by Katherine Drexel and the congregation of the Sisters of the Blessed Sacrament who ran the school. They were dedicated to the education of Native American and African American children. The Sisters welcomed Edward O'Brien in January 1965 to join them and paint the mural "Our Lady of Guadalupe's Love for the

Indian Race." He received only room and board in exchange for the mural at St. Catherine's.

This mural was the second of six murals he painted between 1960 and 1975. Edward O'Brien's use of acrylic paints blended with egg tempera on a dry plastered panel have been compared to those of Renaissance masters because of his minute attention to detail and patient layering of paint and because of the luminosity of the murals. Today, these murals appear as if they were completed recently. His work reflects his study of the Old Masters and their technique of capturing light and expression. In this book I hope to share the excitement I felt upon viewing these murals.

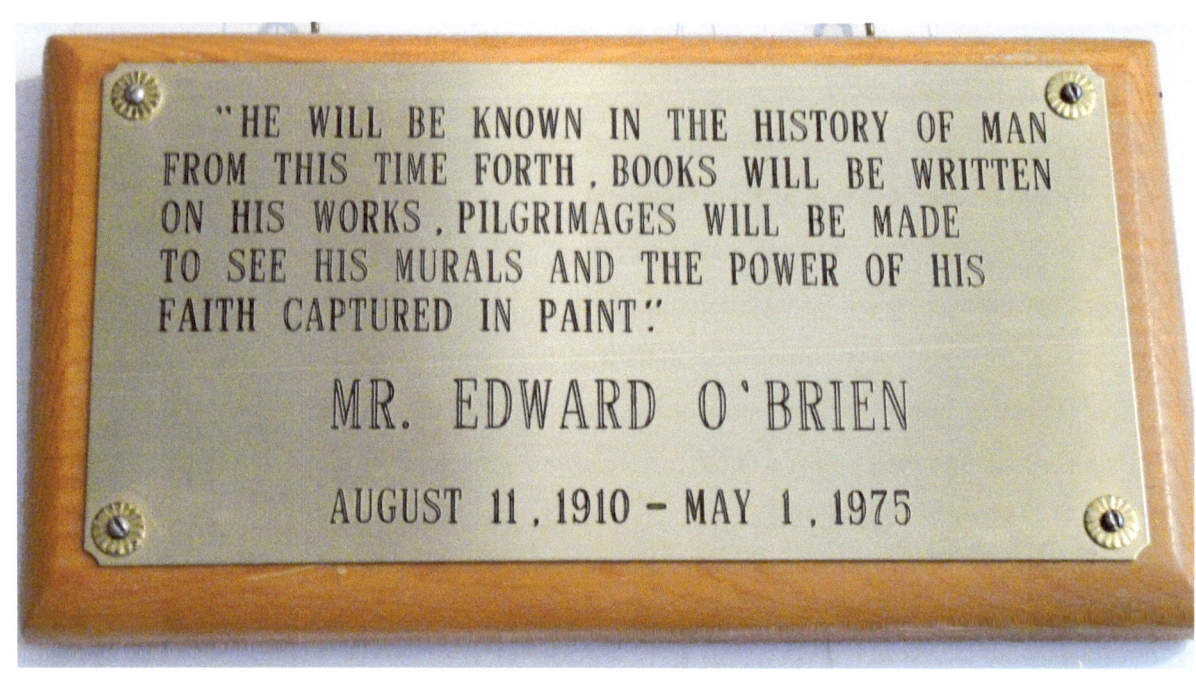

"HE WILL BE KNOWN IN THE HISTORY OF MAN FROM THIS TIME FORTH . BOOKS WILL BE WRITTEN ON HIS WORKS . PILGRIMAGES WILL BE MADE TO SEE HIS MURALS AND THE POWER OF HIS FAITH CAPTURED IN PAINT."

MR. EDWARD O'BRIEN

AUGUST 11 , 1910 – MAY 1 , 1975

Memorial statement from Sikh, Siri Singh Sahib Ji

Edward O'Brien's Life

Edward O'Brien was born August 11, 1910 in Pittsburgh, Pennsylvania of Irish Catholic parents. His father, Edward O'Brien was a merchant in Pennsylvania with a grocery and meat business. His mother, Mary Ann Green O'Brien, was very close to Edward during his life. The parents both died at the age of 62. His four siblings were Gertrude O'Brien Connor, Joseph O'Brien who served in the Navy during World War Two, Mary Ellen O'Brien Vogel whose daughter Carol Vogel was a close friend and associate of Edward's, and Vincent O'Brien who became an ordained Catholic Priest.

Edward began going to art galleries and museums at an early age with his beloved grandfather O'Brien. They explored the city of Pittsburgh together. His grandfather read stories to him and aroused his imagination with tales of Ireland and of his years as a captain on a Mississippi riverboat. He captured Edward's mind and nourished his imagination. They looked at everything from great works of art to butterfly collections. Before Edward was ten, his grandfather died. Edward adored this kind old man and his grandfather's sudden death broke his heart. However, Edward continued to explore art and started to draw constantly, anything and everything. Each Sunday after church, he continued going to art galleries and museums.

At the age of nine, Edward began his study of art at the Diocesan Preparatory School. It was here that the seeds for the future muralist were planted. As a teenager, Edward abandoned thoughts of becoming a priest in favor of studying art and entered Carnegie Tech in Pittsburgh. While at Carnegie Tech he acquired local fame as a sports cartoonist for the *Pittsburgh Post*. His consuming interest was drawing and he began to spend many hours studying theories of design and composition.

1931 found Edward in Chicago, studying at the Art Institute. His passion for art continued, yet he lived as his young adult friends lived enjoying sports, dances, dates, falling in and out of love, and philosophical discussions, lasting far into the night with students, friends and teachers. This philosophical conversation tradition stayed with him for the rest of his life. He lived in a house for students on Lake Shore Drive. There he met John Rheinhardt, professor of English and Latin at Crane College, who became his life-long friend and counselor.

The summer of 1932 was happy and rewarding for Edward, even when the Depression was overtaking the country. Edward left school and joined Professor Rheinhardt at his cabin in the Upper Peninsula of Michigan, a wooded oasis. The cabin had a classical record collection and a library which held the great giants of literature: Aristotle, Plato, Aristophanes, Sophocles, Aquinas, Shakespeare, Cervantes, Tolstoy and Kipling, as well as the poets. For two years he stayed in the woods. John coached him and saw him though a varied and comprehensive curriculum. He worked in lumber camps by day and at night he continued reading, studying and drawing. In 1936 his father died. Edward went home to help with his father's business but did not stay very long and took a job with the WPA heading a government program in which he painted murals in public buildings. He also worked as a stained glass designer and a book illustrator.

World War Two came. Due to a punctured ear drum and an old

back injury all branches of the armed forces rejected him. He took a war industry job and went on with his drawing and studying at night. After the war, Edward tried to get a commission to decorate a church but he and the pastor did not agree on his ideas and he did not get the job. At this time his mother died—his last real contact with home. When he returned home, his family rejected him for not going into the priesthood. It was one of his most hopeless periods. Edward decided to go to Nebraska, to see an old friend, Father Madsen. This kind, perceptive priest commissioned him to paint the Stations of the Cross in St. Mary's Church, outside the little town of Harrison. After completing this commission he left Nebraska.

His whereabouts during the next months are obscure. During this time his thoughts were bitter. His sole purpose was to become a part of the world in which no one in his past life would ever find him. When his money ran out he would ride freights to pick up a little work, earning enough money for his meager needs. Edward roamed the Midwest and finally headed back to Pittsburgh. There he rented a small, inexpensive room. He got a job driving a delivery truck. At night, he went back to drawing, reading and studying philosophy, starting where he had left off.

Edward at this time was influenced by the eighteenth century French cartoon satirist and artist, Honore Daumier. He found in Daumier's satire, irony and compassion in depicting human nature and the human scene, a kindred soul.

Once Edward was settled into his new surroundings, he decided to see an old friend, Clarence Courtney, a talented sculptor. Clarence introduced Edward to Brandon Smith, an architect with whom he was associated. Brandon, eclectic, steeped in Renaissance and Georgian architecture embellished ceilings or walls with old forms conventionalized to meet the needs of the time. He offered Edward a position in his firm. This began a rare and amicable relationship between these three talented men. An architect, a sculptor and a painter! Edward felt an appreciation for this association which would serve him in the future. It was during this period that he completed a major wall mural. When he had time off he painted some portraits and religious egg tempera paintings.

In the summer of 1948, Brandon took Edward with him to meet one of his clients, Margaret Phillips in Western Pennsylvania. He told Edward to bring his recently completed egg tempera painting of the Madonna. They drove up in Brandon's sports car and found Margaret in front of her home waiting for them. After she greeted them in the courtyard, Brandon unwrapped Edward's painting and asked her "What do you think of this?" Edward wandered off to watch her children at play as Brandon and Margaret began discussing the commission that Edward was to work on—her dining room cupboards. Edward was wearing a black turtleneck sweater which, as time went on, became his uniform. When he returned and he and Brandon were getting ready to leave, Margaret offered to buy Edward's painting. It was the first of many that she purchased. Edward did not expect to sell the "Madonna" painting. It was the first work he had executed on his own in many years. Brandon and Margaret agreed on a commission and Edward worked on a project in the Phillips' home for the next three years. He created on the glass panels of their dining room cupboards a series of forty paintings, depicting the history of Western Pennsylvania and the history of farming. They were gems and were very significant in Edward's life as an artist.

The Phillips, especially their children, grew very fond of Edward.

The children adopted him, for he was good and kind and interested in them. His grandfather's influence bore fruit in this special relationship. Their youngest daughter felt a real rapport with him. After school and on many Saturdays he took her on expeditions to Pittsburgh galleries and churches to see paintings and sculptures. Soon she used her own natural artistic instinct and was diligently at work on a mural of her own. Margaret Phillips and Edward also became good friends and she was one of few people in his life with whom he shared his dreams and life experiences. Edward opened her curious mind to the rewards of learning, eventually leading her into the world of writing. The family continued their relationship with Edward after he completed the commission in their home.

Edward returned to Pittsburgh and resigned from his position in the firm formed by Brandon and Clarence. His restless spiritual and personal search for meaning in his life continued and he used his success with Brandon and Clarence to begin an art career with a new confidence. He went to Miami Beach, Florida to fulfill a commission. Opportunities for work were abundant but he made a decision to pursue a spiritual quest. He went to the Trappist Monastery in Kentucky.

There the world slipped away—art, struggle and disillusionment. He was with men who thought, felt and sensed the world as he believed it to be. This was his first of many experiences in a cloister environment. Edward found here solace, peace and a growing relationship with God. At the end of a week he asked to speak to a Novice Master. He was told, "All men, somehow, sometime, must test and prove themselves, if not in, then outside the cloister." Later that evening after compline, Edward read *The Little Flower's Story of a Soul* by St. Therese of Lisieux. *The Little Flower* guided Edward on how to live his life outside the monastery walls. He left the monastery and he went to work as a therapist's assistant in the Industrial Home for Crippled Children in Pittsburgh.

He lived in a small cell-like room. The hours were long and arduous. For two years, in order to perform his duties, he affected insensibility while feeling the pains and sorrows of each child. In time he was able to identify himself with them and appreciated the lesson he had learned in reading *The Little Flower*.

In 1956 his younger brother Vincent was ordained a Catholic priest. Edward was proud of his brother's accomplishment. After the ordination Edward returned to the Home, to the children who had become his children. They loved him. He found joy amusing them with stories and drawings which brought laughter into their lives. He knew now he was not entirely alone. There were people who believed in him. Edward found time to return to his paintings and some of his best portraits and illustrations for several books were done. He uncovered secret methods, techniques and formulas of the Old Masters. This was an accomplishment achieved by few painters. He gained stature as a man working with crippled children and cherished that experience for the rest of his life. It was time to move on.

Edward wanted to investigate the Mexican muralists of Mexico and decided to go to Mexico City to study their mural paintings.

Before his trip to Mexico in 1959, Edward received a letter from his old friend Margaret Phillips. She and her husband had taken a trip to Santa Fe, New Mexico and wrote him that he should consider the "Land of Enchantment" as his next home and to stop there before his return to

Pittsburgh from Mexico. Edward took her advice. He fell in love with Santa Fe, the surrounding countryside, and the people. Believing this area held promise, he left Pittsburgh and moved to Santa Fe.

During Edward's trip to Mexico City in 1959, he may have studied the murals at the San Ildefonso College. It is currently a museum and culture center and considered to be the birthplace of the Mexican muralist movement. In the 1920s the Mexican government sponsored and commissioned the Masters of Mexican mural paintings to paint on the interior walls of the San Ildefonso College. They were Ramon de la Cana, Fermin Revuelatas, Jose Clemente Orozco, Diego Rivera, David Alfaro Siqueiros and Jean Charlot. These mural artists focused on social changes and their effects on the people of Mexico, especially the peasant and Indian populations at the turn of the twentieth century.

The Revolution has been over for many years, but it still exists in its revealing mural paintings: Father Miguel Hidalgo y Costilla, in 1810, with his white locks flying and carrying the banner of Our Lady of Guadalupe as he leads his Indians toward freedom crying, "Long live Our Lady of Guadalupe! Long live Independence"; Zapata and

Villa riding the misty plains and humid forests during the Mexican
Revolution in 1915 with the backs of the peasants as strong as the
Revolution itself, faceless soldiers and their women marching into battle
in a painting by Orozco.

Edward always carried a notebook. The Mexican murals mystified him.
He possibly took note of Diego Rivera. Rivera loved painting—even
more than women and food. Painting was his true love. He painted the
history of Mexico always realistically, sometimes with a savage sense
of caricature and at other times with great compassion for a people
caught up in the tragedy of life. He was a technical master. Edward
was influenced by Diego Rivera and the other Mexican mural masters.
Several years later, Edward depicted early Mexican history in his 1965
mural, "Our Lady of Guadalupe's Love for the Indian Race."

During his study of Mexican murals, Edward took a guided tour
to view Our Lady of Guadalupe on the cloak of Juan Diego at the
Basilica in Mexico City. He had a spiritual enlightenment experience
there and it soon became his mission to spread the devotion to Our
Lady of Guadalupe through his mural paintings. Edward said "At

Guadalupe [Church] I discovered that she was not only the Mother of the Americas, but that she was the Cosmic Mother of the Universe." He stated in an interview shortly before his death, "She is the Mother Principle who gives life to the entire Universe."

It is known that Edward painted murals in different parts of the country. He was a well-read humanist and preferred to paint subjects of a historical and spiritual nature; however, Edward continued to paint portraits and he experimented with landscapes, abstract paintings, and book illustrations after his 1959 trip to Mexico.

In 1960, Edward arrived in Santa Fe, New Mexico and was recognized as a master mural artist. Providentially, he was offered the opportunity to meet Merle Armitage, an author of more than 30 books, art critic and Art Director of *Look* Magazine. Merle was introduced to Edward by Margaret Phillips. They immediately became friends and collaborators. Merle hired Edward to be the illustrator for his book *Pagans, Conquistadores, Heroes and Martyrs* published in 1960. Edward was offered also a commission to paint a mural, setting into motion events which changed his life.

Edward's whole concept of what an artist could accomplish was enriched by his friendship with Merle Armitage. They often took trips into New Mexico's wilderness where Edward sketched and painted landscapes. Merle also encouraged Edward to experiment in abstract paintings. New Mexico was Edward's new home until his death in 1975.

In 1964 Merle Armitage published a book on Edward O'Brien's life entitled *Painter into Artist: The Progress of Edward O'Brien* as recorded by Margaret Phillips and Merle Amitage. In 1963, Merle also wrote an article in *The Santa Fe New Mexican* celebrating the unveiling of Edward's mural "Our Lady of Light" at the Loretto Academy School for Girls in Santa Fe, New Mexico.

There are six murals that have been recognized as works Edward O'Brien produced during the last fifteen years of his life. Four murals were painted in New Mexico; one mural was completed in Benet Lake, Wisconsin and one in Chicago, Illinois. Each of these murals took two to three years to complete. He may have continued his portrait art work as well.

Edward's first commission in New Mexico was for the Loretto Academy High School in Santa Fe. It was a mural of "Our Lady of Light" and its unveiling took place September 8, 1963. Critics of the time who had seen the mural believed it was one of the most important works of art in the Southwest. The Loretto Academy High School closed its doors in 1969. The mural of "Our Lady of Light" was moved in the early 1970s to a private chapel in Tesuque, New Mexico. In the late 1990s, the mural was once again moved. It was donated to Los Hermanos Penitentes for their *morada* in La Madera, New Mexico. The mural needed to be cut in half in order to get it into the *morada*. It was pieced together; however, the one inch cut needs restoration at the time of the publication of this book. The rest of the beautiful mural is in good condition.

Following this work, Edward began the mural at St. Catherine's Indian School in January 1965 in Santa Fe, New Mexico. He called the mural "Our Lady of Guadalupe's Love for the Indian Race." The 19 ¼' x 10 ½' colorful, floor-to-ceiling work depicts ten significant events affecting the indigenous peoples of the Americas. Our Lady of Guadalupe is at the center of the mural. It was completed after it was formally dedicated June 18, 1966, by Bishop William Connare of Greensburg, Pennsylvania. The models O'Brien used to paint the portraits in the mural were students, sisters, brothers and priests who were at the school. Reverend Mother Katherine and Mother Mercedes had prominent places in the completed mural. St. Catherine's Indian School was closed in 1998. The main building where this mural is located is protected under the New Mexico State Register of Cultural properties and there is a citizens' group that supports the protection and preservation of this important New Mexico art treasure.

At the Benedictine, Our Lady of Guadalupe Abbey in Pecos, New Mexico, Edward O'Brien was commissioned to paint a mural depicting stories of appearances of the Holy Mother. In the center is Our Lady of Guadalupe. Saint Bernadette is on the left of Our Lady of Guadalupe. At fourteen, Saint Bernadette is said to have experienced eighteen visions of the Holy Mother. On the right of Our Lady of Guadalupe are children looking up at Our Lady of Fatima who appears on the top of a tree. Above this image is Saint Catherine Laboure who was part of the Daughters of Charity of Saint Vincent de Paul at Chatillonsur-Seine, France in 1830. The Holy Mother appeared to her once in the form of a picture standing on a globe. The picture turned around and on the reverse side appeared a capital M with a cross above it and two hearts, one thorn-crowned and the other pierced with a sword. The Holy Mother asked Saint Catherine to have a medal made of the image, promising that all who wore the medal would receive great graces. This medal is known to Catholics as the "Miraculous Medal." It is painted in the center of the top of the mural.

Edward's next work took him away from his beloved New Mexico surroundings and he spent the next three years at the St. Benedict's Abbey in Benet Lake, Wisconsin. Here he diverted from the image of Our Lady of Guadalupe and created a mural in their Monastery Retreat Center Dining Room, entitled "Christ in Man." The images are all important men mainly from the Old Testament as well as an image of John the Baptist. At the center of the mural is an image of a beardless young Christ. Edward also depicts in the mural Heaven and Earth, Bread/Eucharist and symbols of the major religions in the world. It was completed in 1969. Edward lived among the Abbey's Brothers. Father Geraets said "Ed would work into the night until he was exhausted." When he took time off he would join the brothers and have many individual talks and philosophical discussions.

Edward's fifth mural commission was for the Catholic Parish of St. Pius V in Chicago, Illinois. This mural was painted on a curved wall and was titled "The Mother of the Americas" in honor of the Latin American population. The Mexican-American congregation commissioned the mural as part of its centennial celebration. In the mural under Christ's spreading arms, light radiates from Our Lady of Guadalupe. At the left, Mexican history begins its march from ancient to modern times; at the right, figures from theology and miracles mingle with the typical Mexican family in the foreground. The father, mother, and daughter are modeled after three members of the St. Pius V congregation. Edward said the artistic concept for the mural came to him in an Indian kiva in New Mexico. He may have made a trip back to New Mexico before he started this mural. It was completed in 1972.

Upon Edward's return to Santa Fe, New Mexico in the early 1970s, he met some young American Sikhs in Pecos, New Mexico who wanted to view his mural at the St. Benedict's Abbey. They discussed with him the image of "Our Lady of Guadalupe" and how She compared to the feminine principle in Sikh Dharma. Edward realized there was a connection between this principle and his spiritual interpretation of Our Lady of Guadalupe. He asked them about their religious faith, Sikh Dharma, and later he agreed to create a mural for them at the Sikh Ashram. The mural represents the history of the Sikh religion.

Edward started the Sikh mural in 1973 at his studio off Canyon Road where he began the center mural panel painting of "Our Lady of Guadalupe." When it was ready he had it shipped to the Sikh Ashram where he joined it between the two other blank mural panels already in place at the Ashram. Edward then decided to move into the Sikh Ashram in Espanola, New Mexico where he lived until the mural's completion.

The mural painting depicts fire, water, plant life, animal life, and family life. On each side the of Our Lady of Guadalupe are the Sikh Gurus in chronological order, and next to them is a detailed painting of each man's major virtue or a significant event in his life. Edward completed the mural in late April, 1975.

Edward drew the attention of the head of the Sikh religion in the Western hemisphere, Yogi Bhajan, who requested that he do a mural for the Golden Temple in Amrit Sar, India. Unfortunately, on May 1, 1975, one week after Edward finished the mural in Espanola, New Mexico, he died of a heart attack at the Sikh Center. It was a loss to the community. The Sikh leader gave this eulogy: "He will be known in the history of man from this time forth. Books will be written on his works. Pilgrimages will be made to see his murals and the power of his faith captured in paint."

Edward O'Brien was a Catholic but was noted for his spirituality and openness to other religions and friendships with men and women of all faiths. He enjoyed reading historical, philosophical and inspirational books. He was a spiritual and humble man. He never married nor had children. Edward O'Brien's surviving family—brothers, Joseph, Father Vincent, S.J. and Edward's friend and niece Carol Vogel attended his funeral. His brother, Father Vincent M. O'Brien, S.J. celebrated the Mass at his funeral.

Edward O'Brien's remains were transferred to the St. Catherine's
Indian School in Santa Fe, New Mexico for the funeral May 5, 1975.
Sister Catherine said "The funeral was a blend of Christian ritual,
Indian and Spanish music and the thought of the East. Ed O'Brien
was known and respected by people who came from all over to pay him
tribute. He was laid out in our room in front of his mural 'Our Lady
of Guadalupe's Love for the Indian Race' with the Virgin looking
down on him, and is buried here in the Sister's little cemetery, but I
think his work speaks to his faith better than any of us ever could."

His death was a great sorrow to those close to him. In memory of
Edward O'Brien on May 5, 1985, the Governor of New Mexico,
Toney Anaya, proclaimed it Edward O'Brien Day.

Edward O'Brien's Murals
1960–1975

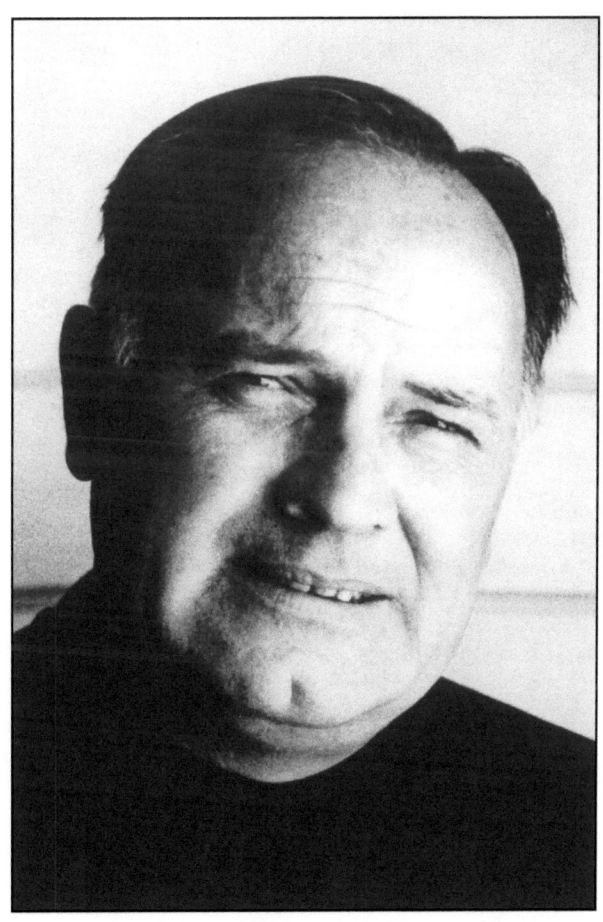

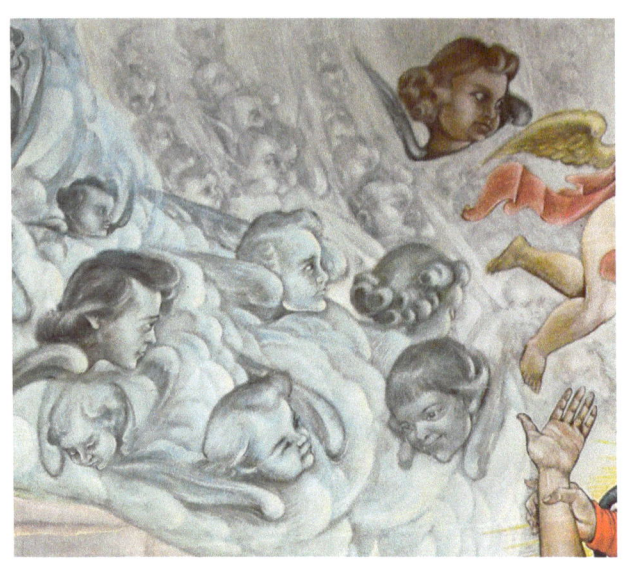

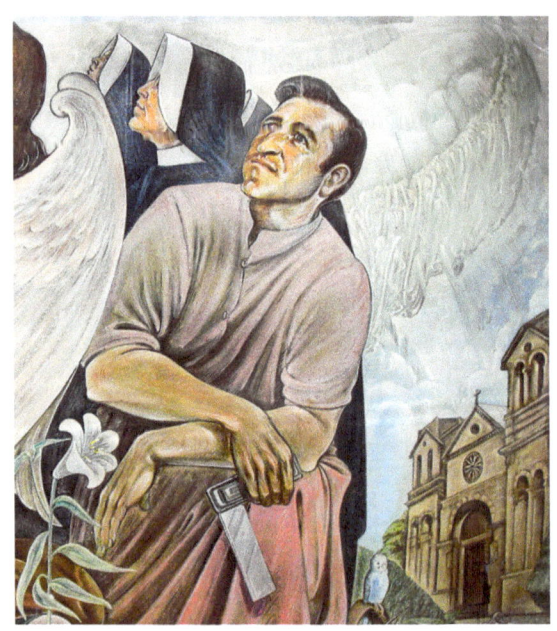

34

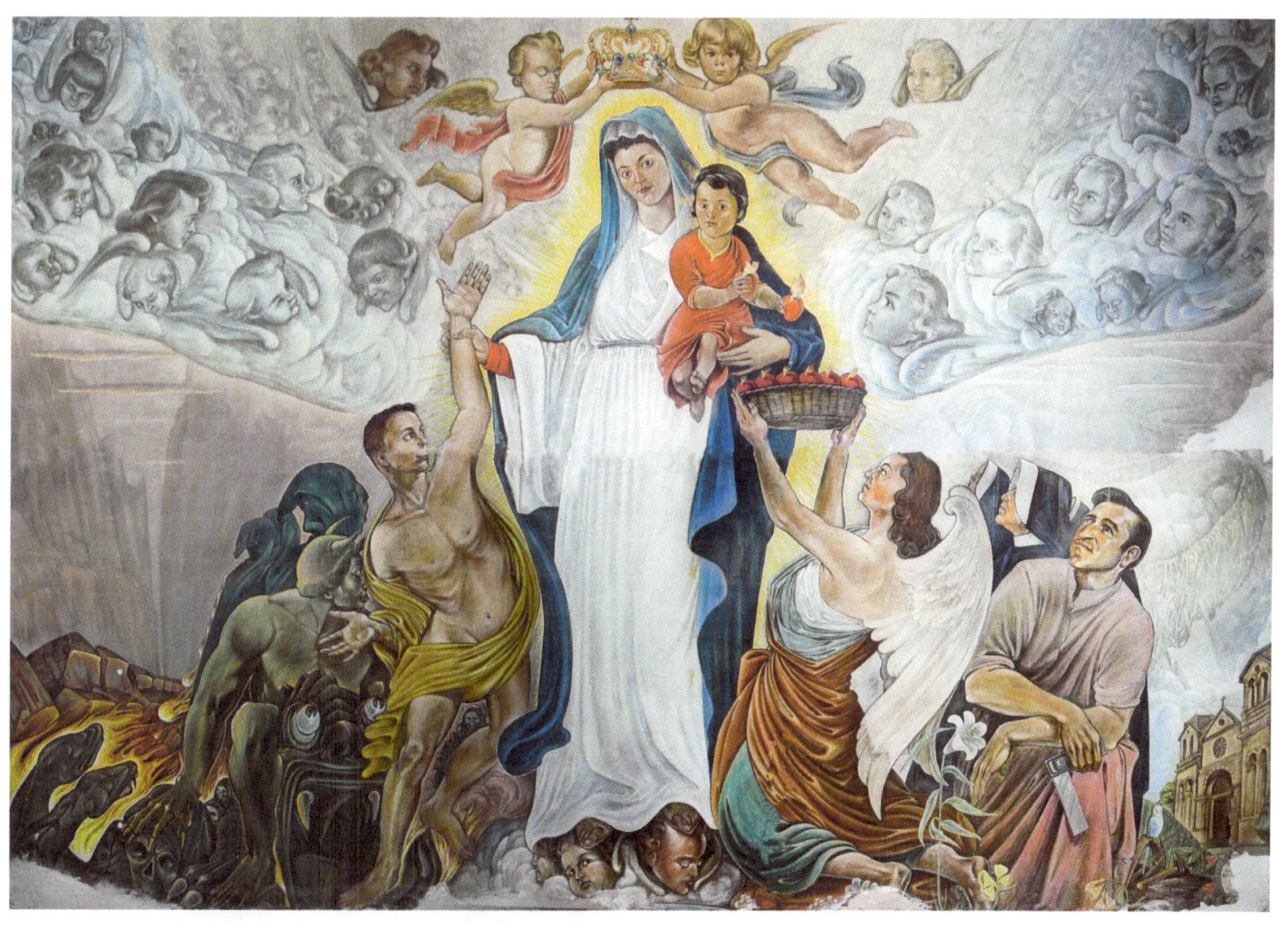

Our Lady of Light (1963)
Courtesy of Los Hermanos Penitentes morada, La Madera, New Mexico
Photograph by Peter E. Lopez

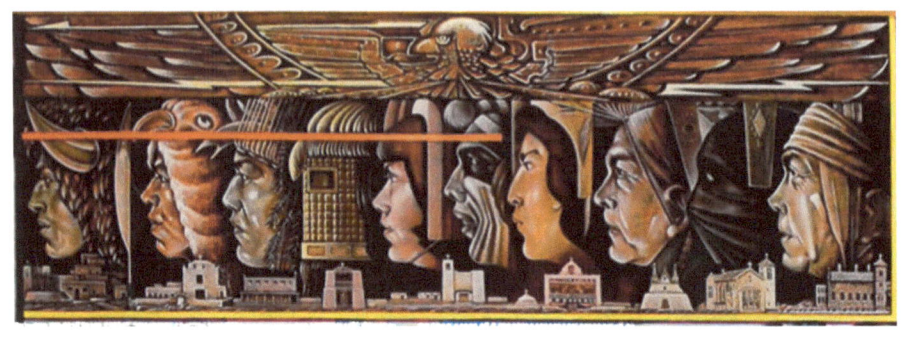

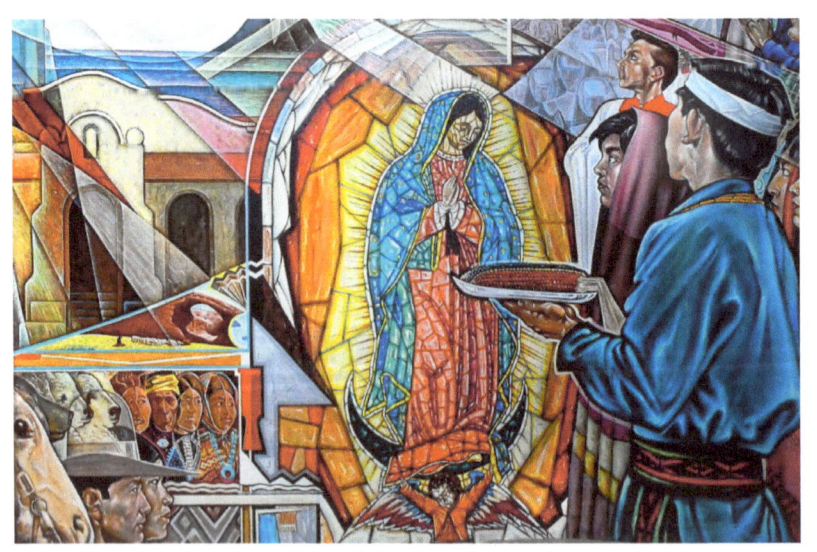

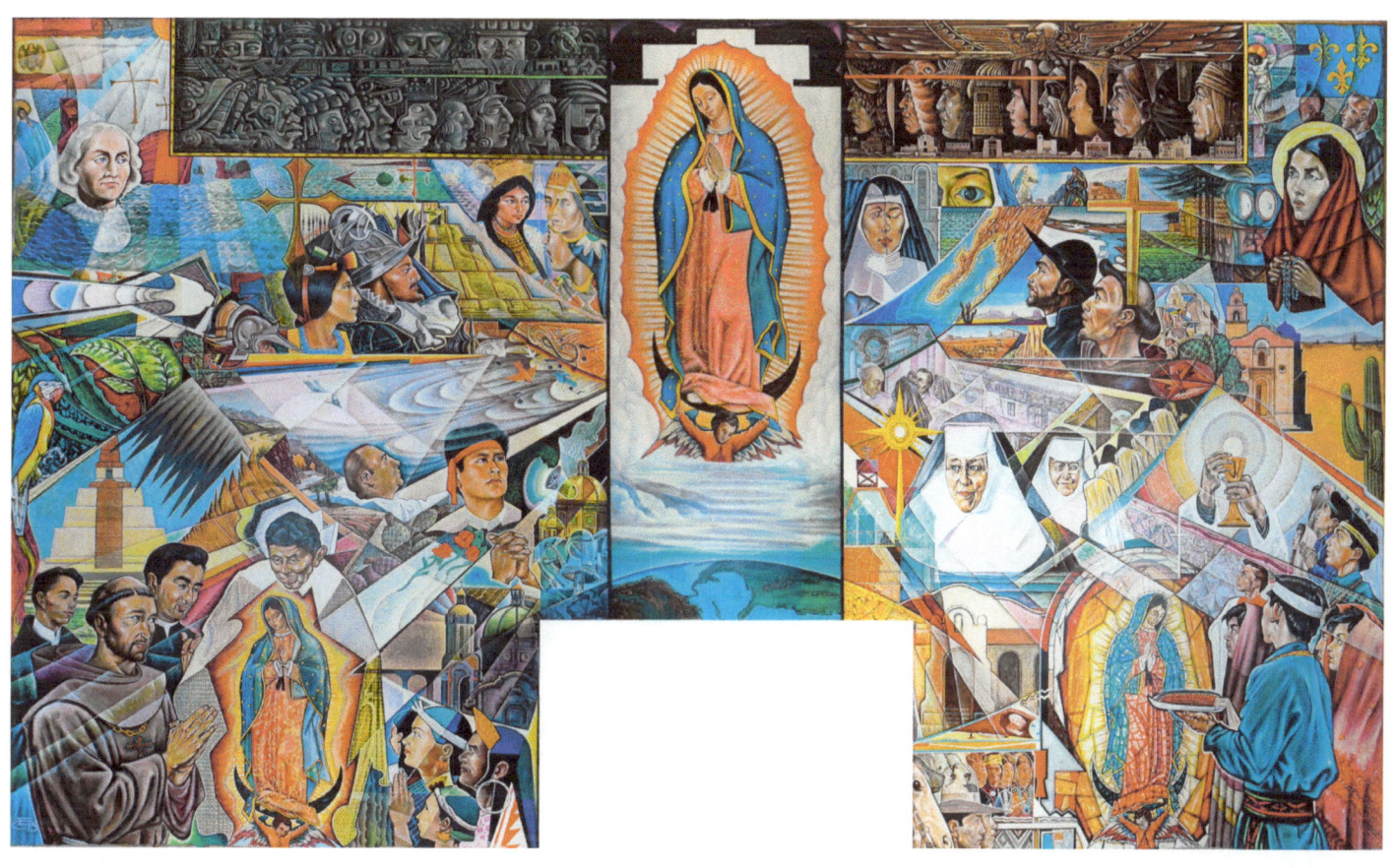

Our Lady of Guadalupe's Love for the Indian Race (1966)
Courtesy of Mr. and Mrs. Max Tafoya, St. Catherine's Indian School, Santa Fe, New Mexico
Photograph by Peter E. Lopez

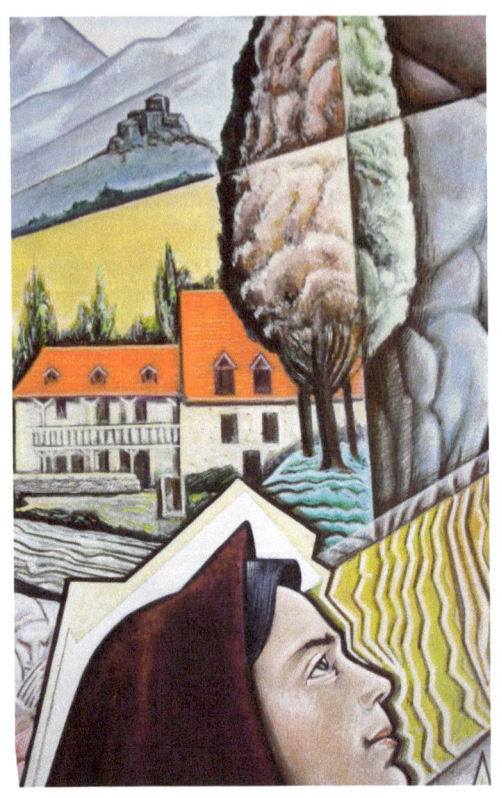

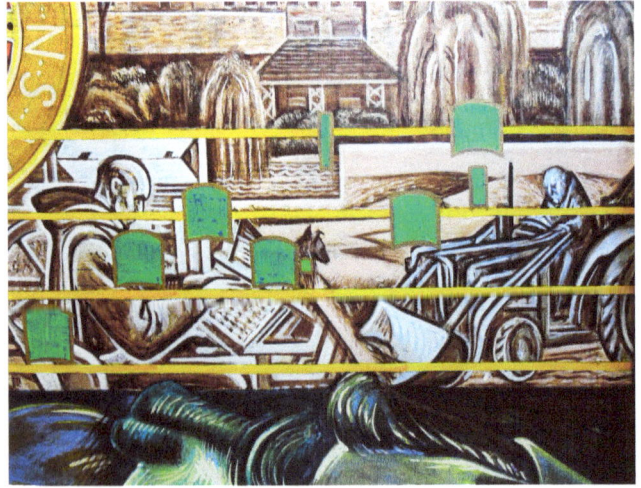

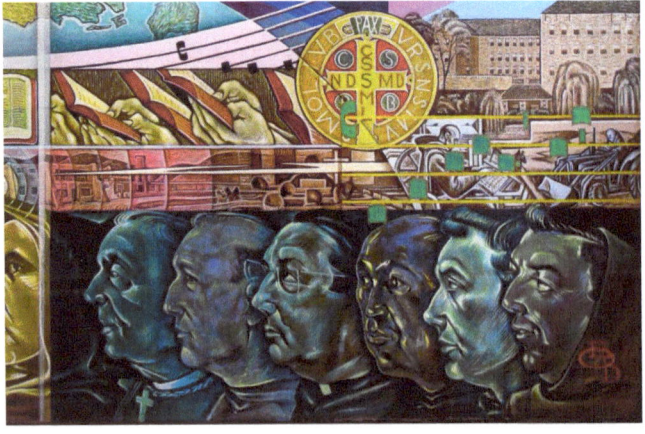

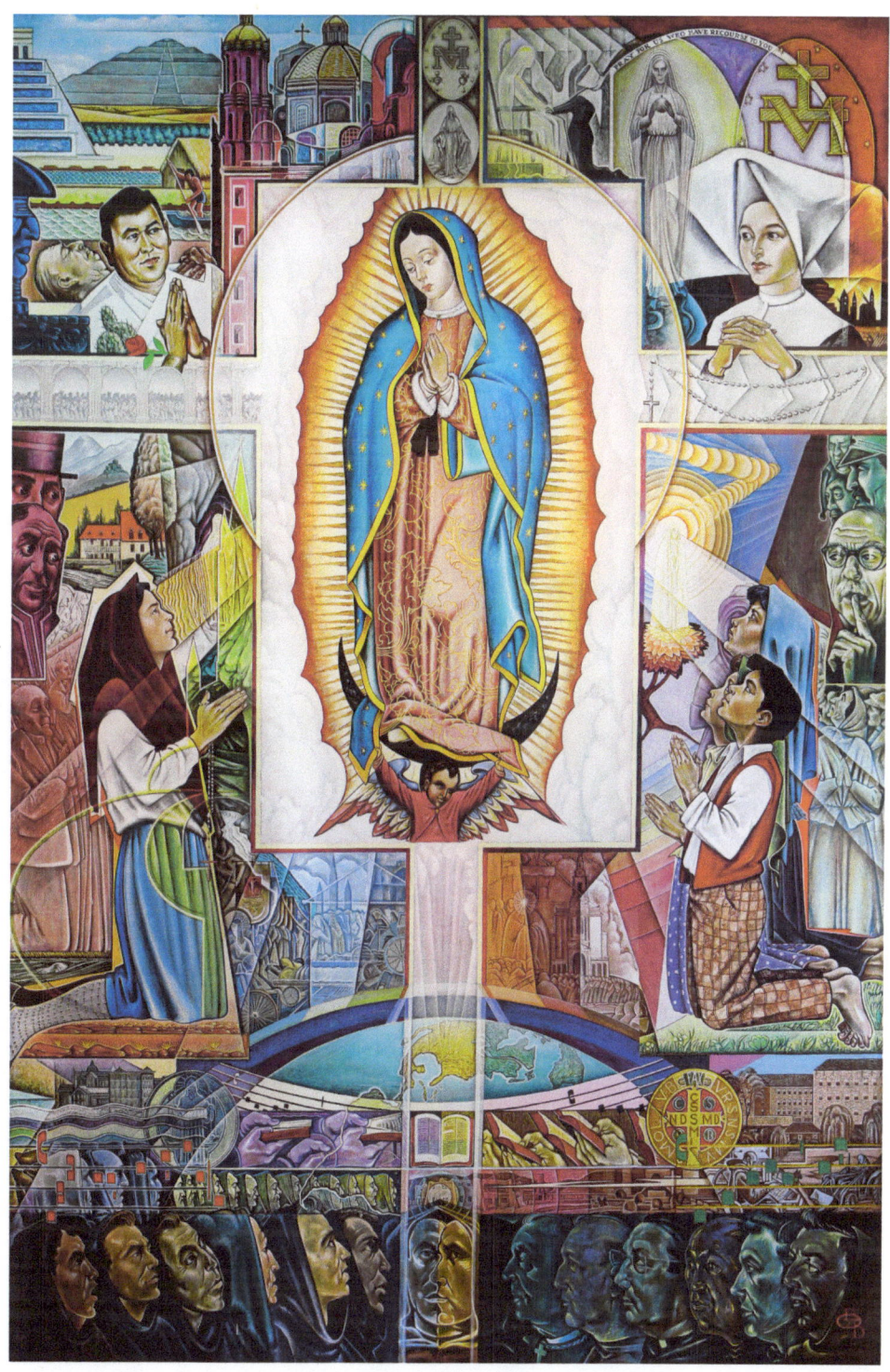

Our Lady of Guadalupe (1967)

Courtesy of Our Lady of Guadalupe
Abbey, Pecos, New Mexico

Photograph by Peter E. Lopez

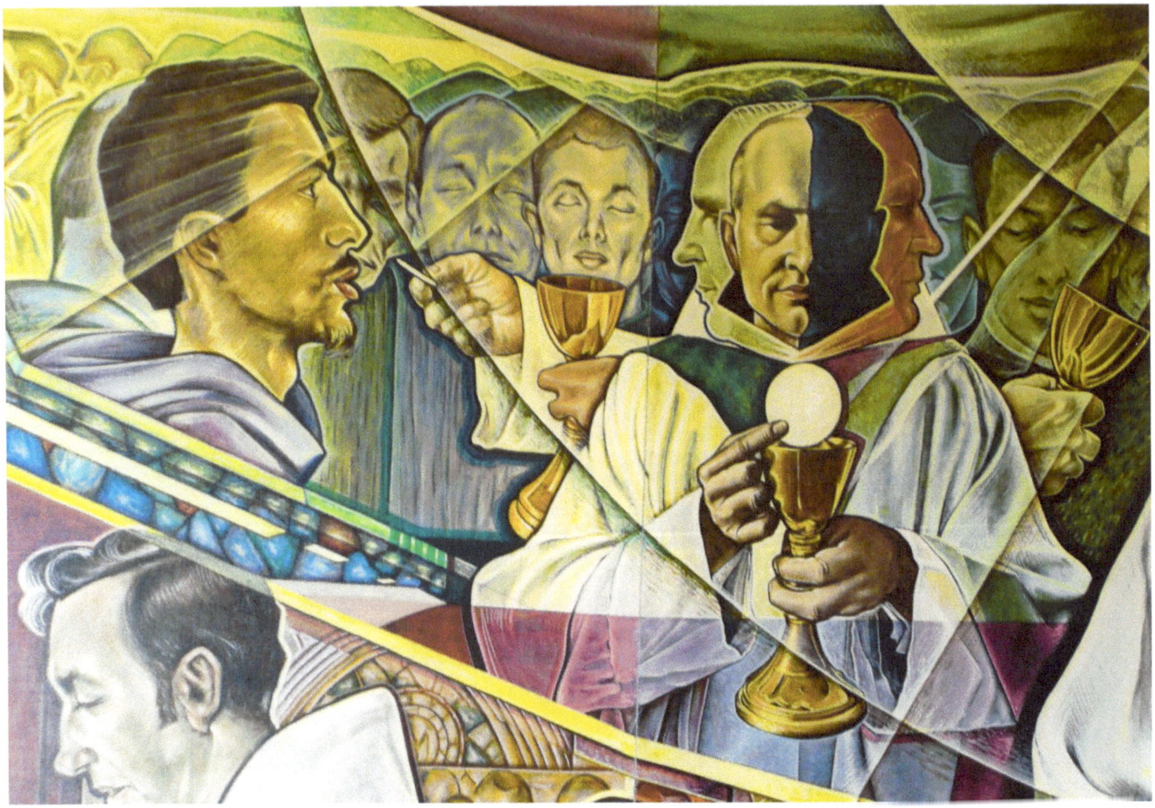

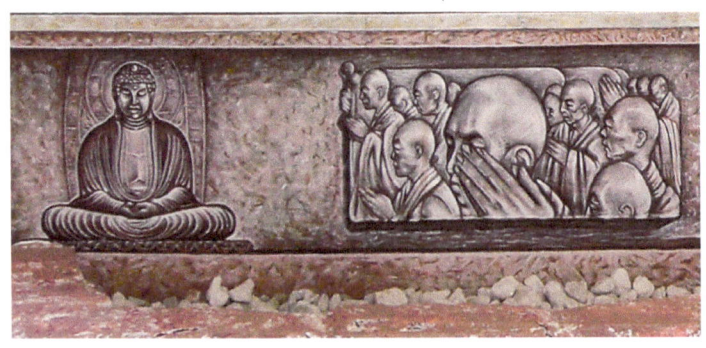

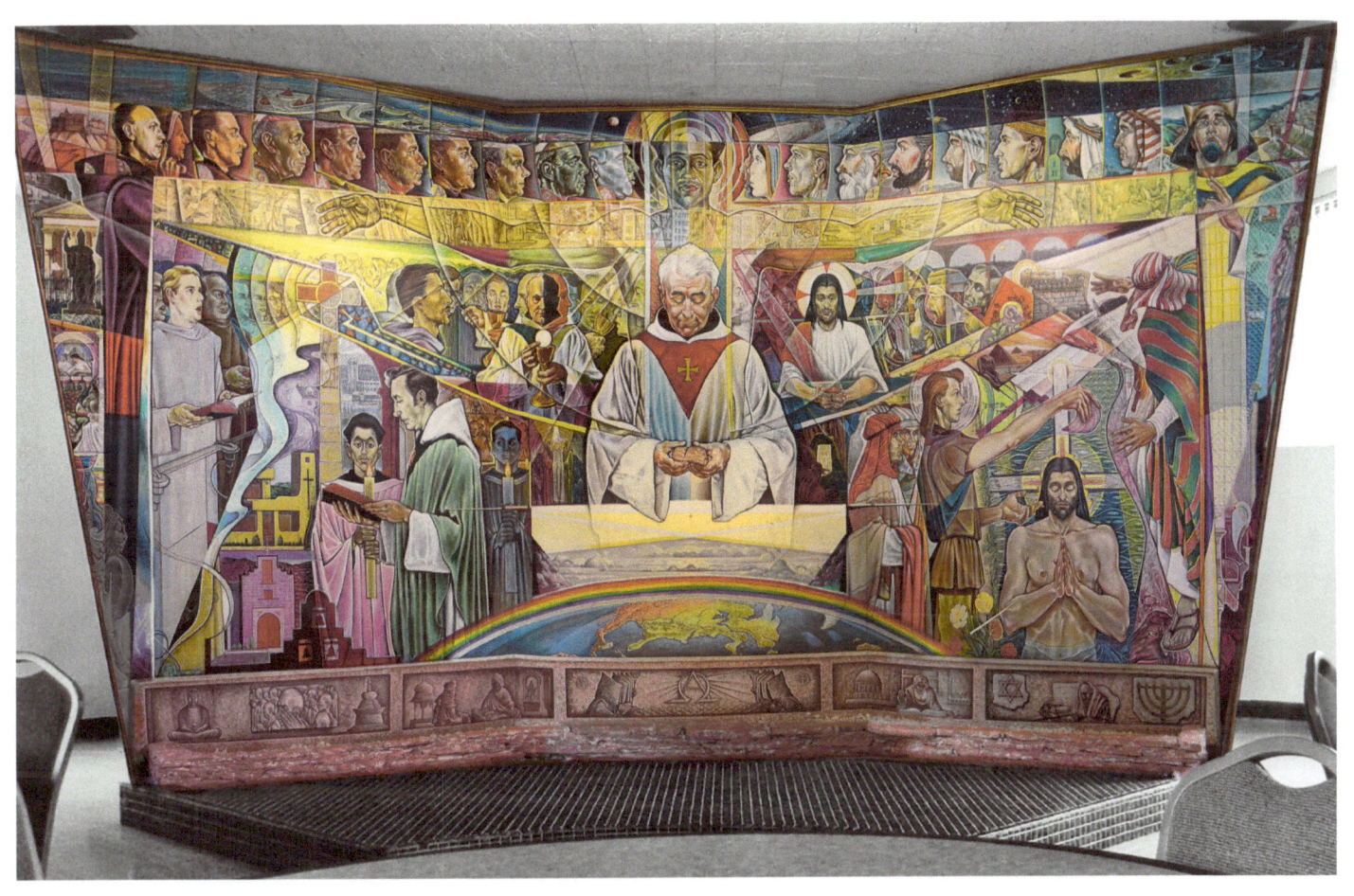

Christ In Man (1969)
Courtesy of St. Benedict's Abbey, Benet Lake, Wisconsin
Photograph by Father Kevin Murphy

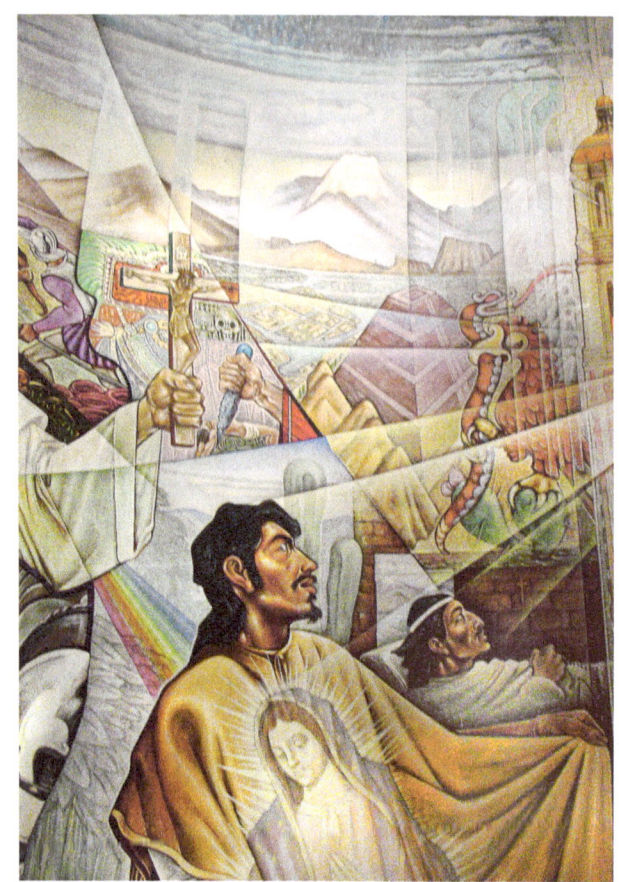

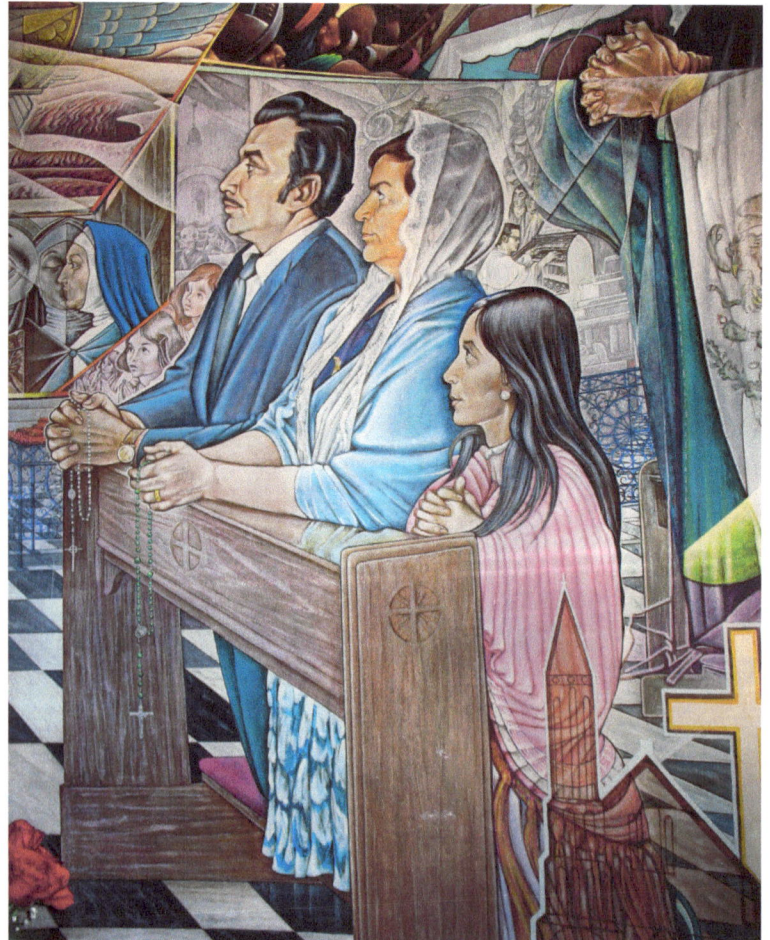

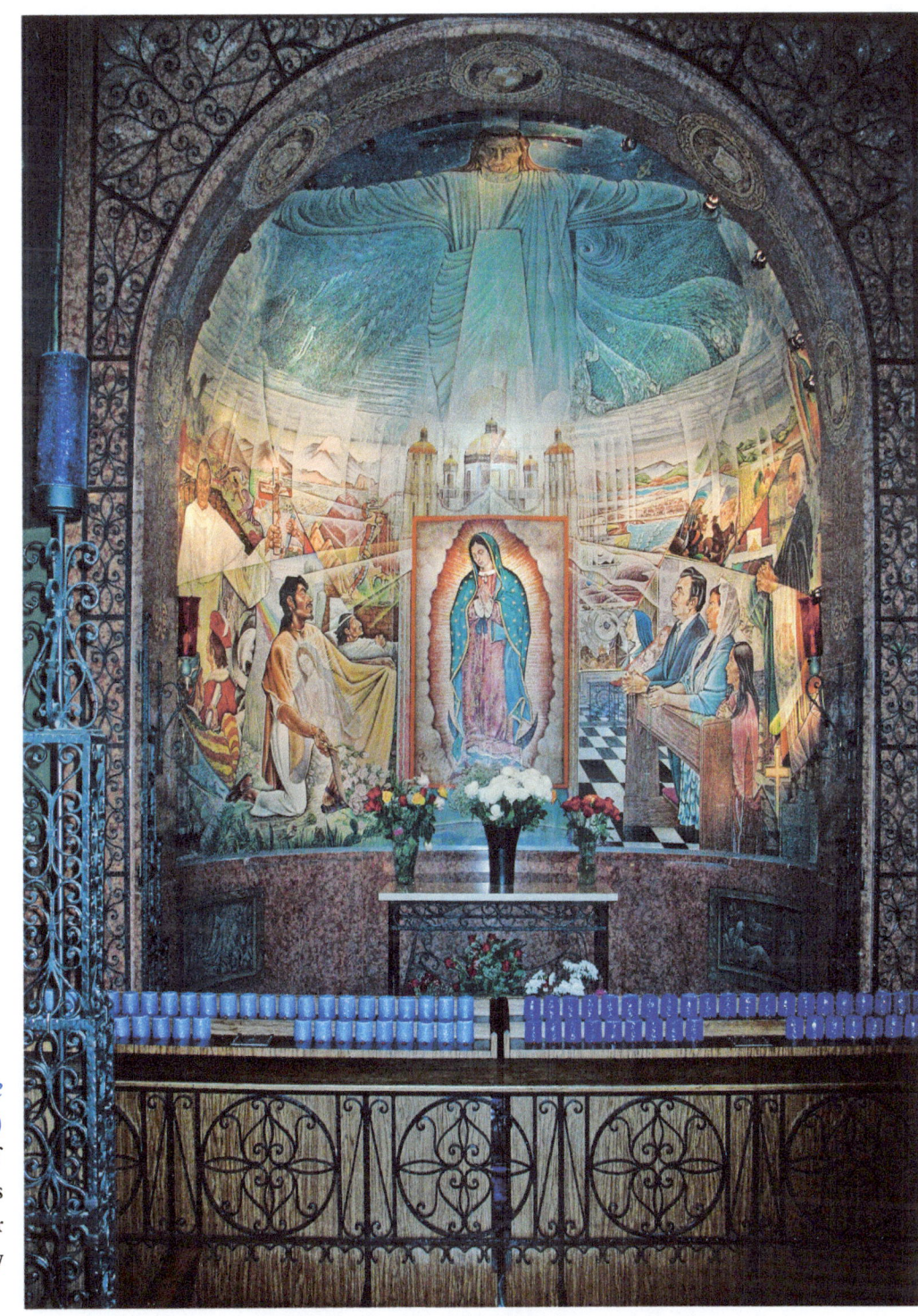

The Mother of the Americas (1972)
Courtesy of the Catholic Parish of
St. Pius V, Chicago, Illinois
Photograph by Brother
Malachy McCarthy

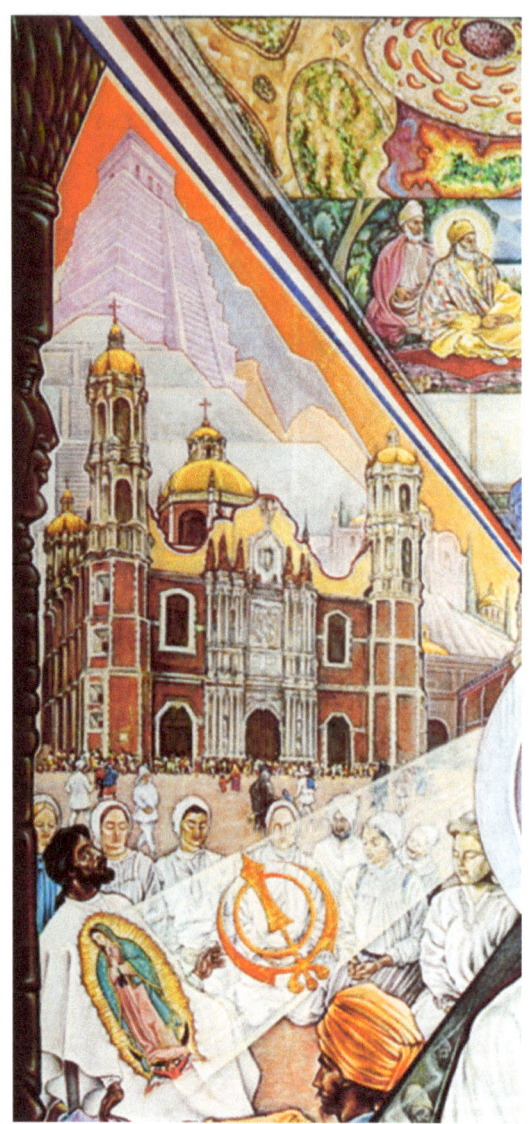

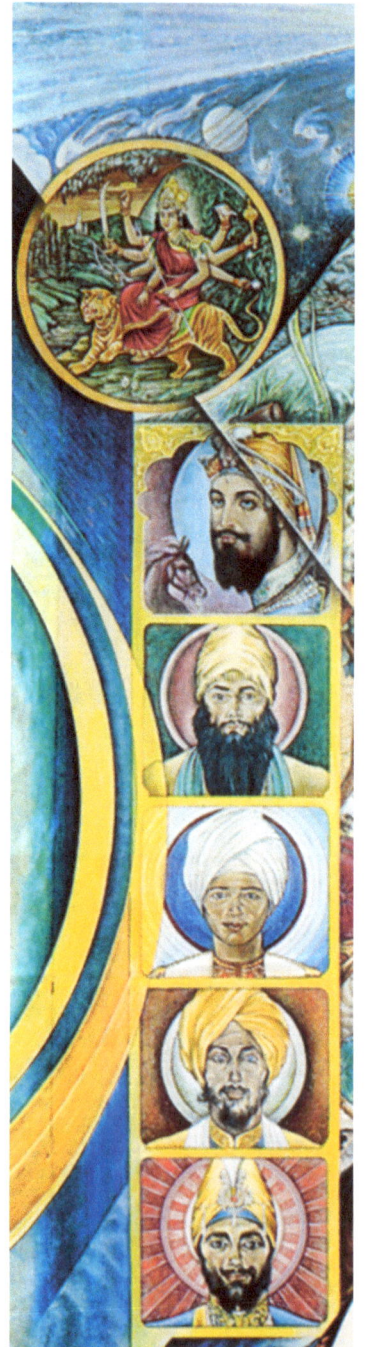

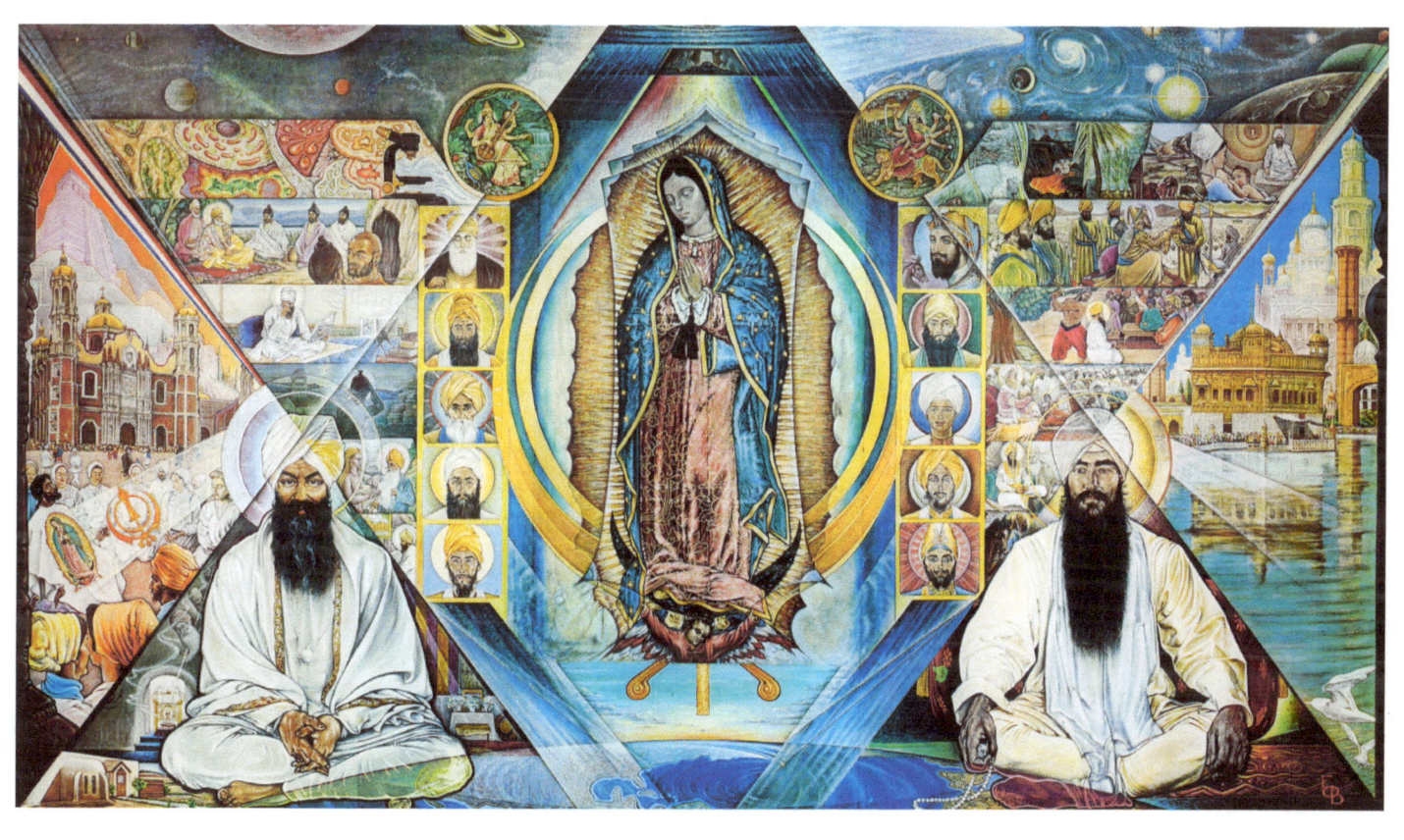

Our Lady of Guadalupe (1975)
Courtesy of Hacienda de Guru Ram Das, Espanola, New Mexico
Photograph by Peter E. Lopez

Acknowledgments

I want to express my sincere gratitude to the following: first and foremost, Werner Buhlmann a Graphic Designer in Zurich, Switzerland, who encouraged me to document the life and artwork of Edward O'Brien; Dr. Judith Land, Montezuma, New Mexico, for her editorial support, love and friendship; Barbara Tafoya, Albuquerque, New Mexico, who first introduced me to the mural art work of Edward O'Brien; Guru Meher Kaur, Gurnam Kaur and Mukhtiar Singh, from the Sikh Ashram in Espanola, New Mexico, who guided me; Daniel Gurule, Santa Fe, New Mexico, friend of Edward O'Brien; Roberto Montoya, member of Los Hermanos Penitentes de La Madera, New Mexico; Elaine Bergman, Executive Director of The Historic Santa Fe Foundation, Santa Fe, New Mexico; Devon Skeele, Librarian, New Mexico Museum of Art, Santa Fe, New Mexico; Patricia Hewitt, Senior Cataloguer Fray Angelico Chavez History Library, Santa Fe, New Mexico; Tim Greer, Librarian Director, Santa Fe Public Library, Santa Fe, New Mexico;

Brother John M. Davies, Benedictine Monastery, Pecos, New Mexico;
Fr. Kevin Murphy, St. Benedict's Abbey, Benet Lake, Wisconsin;
Malachy McCarthy, Claretian Mission Archives, Chicago, Illinois;
Fr. David Geraets, Monastery of the Risen Christ, San Luis Obispo,
California; Fr. Chuck Dahm, St. Pius V Parish, Chicago, Illinois;
Dr. Stephanie Morris Director of Archives, Sisters of the Blessed
Sacrament, Bensalem, Pennsylvania; and the surviving family members
of Edward O'Brien; Carol Vogel, Webster, New York, Edward's
niece and friend who gave me the direction into Edward O'Brien's past
life; Rev. Vincent M. O'Brien, S.J., Merion Station, Pennsylvania,
youngest brother of Edward O'Brien who loaned me the important
recorded memoirs of Margaret Phillips in 1964 (*Painter into Artist:
the Progress of Edward O'Brien* as recorded by Margaret Phillips and
Merle Armitage. Manzanita Press, 1964); and *The Santa Fe New
Mexican* Archives.

Sponsors (as of the publication date of this book):

Gurufateh Khalsa

John and Martha Spencer

Judith Land

Werner and Helen Muller

Alice L. Sandoval

Theresa "Titi" Felix

Matilda Rivera

Lenore and Calvin Bockbrader

Dr. and Mrs. Alfred J. Martin, Jr.

Patricia and Edwin J. Ducayet, Jr.

Beverly and Don Freeman

Guru Meher and Noor Khalsa

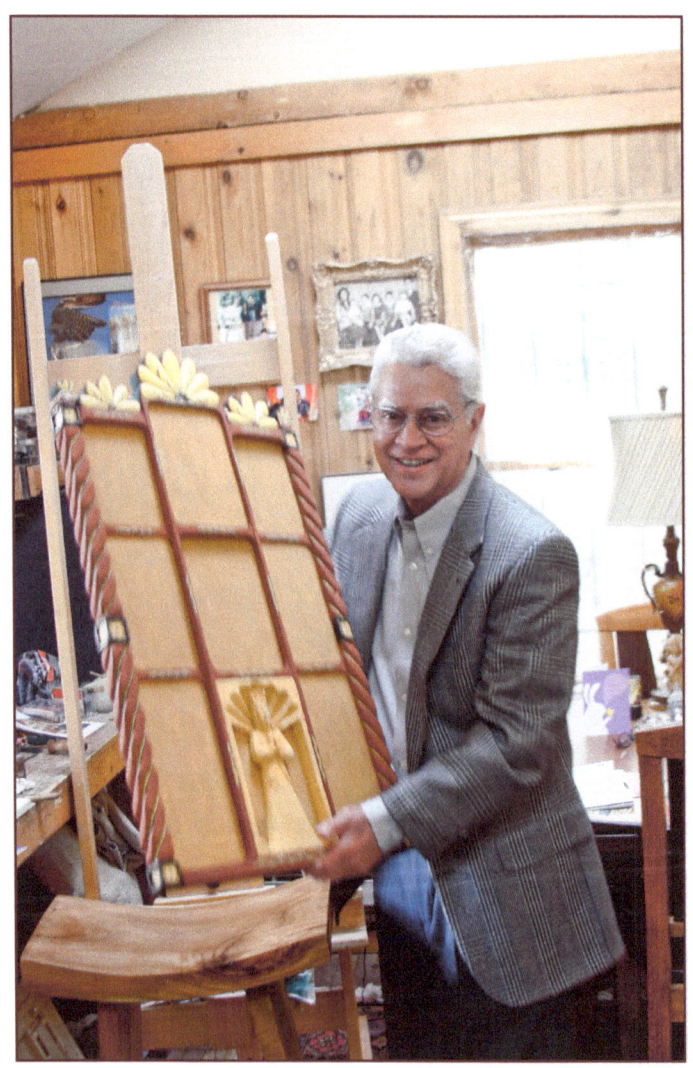

Photograph by Arjan Stockhausen

About the Author

Peter Lopez wrote this book to revive interest and attention to the contributions of Edward O'Brien's life and mural art. Over the course of a year Peter conducted interviews with a variety of people from the monks of various Benedictine orders, priests, friends, family and associates of the artist.

Peter himself is a santero artist who has a background in researching the lives of the various saints he has depicted in his artwork. He is a respected artist who has won top awards during his twenty year association with the Spanish Colonial Arts Society of Santa Fe, New Mexico. He graduated from the University of New Mexico with a Bachelor of Arts in Art Education. He resides in the small community of Montezuma, New Mexico.

www.ingramcontent.com/pod-product-compliance
Lightning Source LLC
Chambersburg PA
CBHW050901180526

45159CB00007B/2751